Confessions of a Sixties Mom

Confessions of a Sixties Mom

by G.Joy Robins

First Edition: September 2015
Printed in the United States of America

This book is dedicated to my niece, Melody Rose Robins Shaw, now known as Isis. Her skills and love have helped release me from my demons enabling me to share my story.

Dear Luise,

Good sitting next to you in class!

Love, Joy

G. Joy Robins

Table of Contents

Introduction

I have long had the ambition of writing a book but I hesitated. I hardly ever read fiction. Most of what I read is History, which includes autobiographies or better still, Archaeology, which is history so old it has to be put together from clues.

What do I have to contribute? When I worked on a title, I settled on "Confessions of a Sixties Mom". I think it is apt in many ways. I finally feel free to "confess" things I felt guilt about, with the new perspective my encounter with my niece Isis has provided me.

Why "sixties mom"? I was profoundly empowered and changed by the shift in societal values that the sixties symbolize. We liked things that were down to earth and not pretentious. The return to folk music included much that protested against injustice and inequity. I personally did not participate in the "sex, drugs and rock and roll". I was in a bad marriage and not getting much sex. I was afraid even to drink and didn't smoke, so drugs did not attract me.

The part about Civil Rights did attract me, but I was home doing diapers. The disposable kind existed but they were very expensive. I had a diaper service for only a very short time. Then we got a washer and dryer in the basement. I rinsed cloth diapers in the toilet and washed them in the basement when I could get time to go down there. I hated it.

The sixties movement that I completely related to was "Women's Lib", which refers to the liberation of women. It took me some time to break free from my bonds but I was a Feminist and so were my mother and grandmother before me.

I have a Masters in Child Development and worked as a Social Worker and Family Therapist but it is my experience helping myself, in an effort to help my daughters and my niece, that has made me who I am.

That is basically what pulls this book together. It is the story of four generations of the women of one family and their struggle toward full independent personhood. It starts at the turn of the 20th century and brings us into the 21st.

Since I am beyond becoming a writer as a career or impressing anyone with being a writer, it doesn't make much sense to write a book. This is more of a continuation of me having my say on facebook. I love facebook. I have been enjoying the antics of an adorable, bright little girl and the sayings of a facebook friend's precocious son. I have been watching some wonderful young adults navigate their time of life with enthusiasm and sometimes despair. I have become very fond of a high school mate that I still haven't met in person. She paints and I like her style.

This all started when my middle daughter Holly offered to get this book published. That is the easy part these days. You can get your laundry list published, if you are willing and able to pay. Getting readers is another thing altogether.

My oldest daughter, Regina, I still call her "Gigi", her childhood nickname, then offered to be my Editor. That has also included Researcher, since she volunteered to be our Ancestry.com connection. She has always been the one curious about our origins.

She is named after my maternal grandmother, Regina Goldstein (later Gold) Blumer. That Regina, my nana, liked the name but complained that people called her Reggie, which she hated. When I named my first child for her, I installed a very nice nickname so she would never have to worry about being called Reggie.

My youngest daughter, Miriam, was called Mickey since she was a baby. She liked that, even though she had a lyrical biblical name. She eventually decided to spell it Mikki. Now that she is an adult, she also uses Miriam. She has been the keeper of many of the family's old photos. Thanks to her, this book has some really good illustrations.

My only niece, Melody Rose Robins Shaw, had a perfectly beautiful first name, but it didn't suit her. She reinvented herself and took the name of the Egyptian Goddess, Isis. Unfortunately in recent years a terrorist group has been labeled that by our media, even though they don't call themselves that. Hopefully, they will be gone and forgotten before long.

Isis is a whiz at producing videos. The growth process that led to this effort started when I took a "pod cast" course that she produced.

Maybe I will be able to persuade her to make a video of me or maybe even her, reading some of the juicer parts of this book, complete with appropriate music. If she agrees, and it goes viral, my readership problem may be solved. She lives in the Pacific Northwest. I might have to learn to use Skype.

Chapter One

History

I was born on July 16, 1936. In 1945 they chose my birthday to test the first Atomic bomb.

I have lived long enough for my search for myself to have succeeded, only recently of course. Now I better understand the story of my life and how it is intertwined with the stories of the lives of my loved ones and even some of my relatives that I never knew. Many stories are played out over more than one generation.

My mother had a secret that she kept to the grave. It is interesting that I found it out because of Google, almost by accident. My daughter Gigi looked up my Uncle Jack (Jacob Blumer, AKA Jon L. Blummer).

My mother's older brother had gotten a few more than his 15 minutes of fame. He was a commercial artist and drew "Hop Harrigan" the comic strip and later radio show of the 1940s. It didn't last far into the 50's.In spite of Hop's attempt at being a "Cold Warrior". The daring pilot Hop and his mechanic sidekick Tank Tinker just didn't adapt well to peacetime.

When the article came up, it was a research piece about Jon L. Blummer that also mentioned my maternal grandmother, my nana, Regina Blumer. It is on line under Field guide to Wild American Pulp Artists, www.pulpartists.com/Blummer.html .

> *"In 1909 his father founded The Blumer College of Naturopathy, of which his father was President, Dean, Professor, as well as a practicing Doctor, who treated visiting patients. His mother was the school secretary. The school ran advertisements in local newspapers.*
>
> *In 1911 newspaper advertisements for the school began to describe his father as a Doctor of Psychology as well as Naturopathy.*
>
> *In 1918 during the Great War he was fourteen and a student in the ninth grade,*

so he was too young for military service. In 1922 he graduated Hartford High School.

In December 6, 1923 as a result of Connecticut Grand Jury investigation of medical fraud, Hartford Deputy Sheriffs raided the Blumer College of Naturopathy.

After a struggle with Dr. Blumer and twenty-four students, all the school's accounts, ledgers and papers were seized, including Dr. Blumer's checkbook. The Connecticut State Council of Health revoked the licenses of twenty-five doctors for holding repudiated diplomas.

One week later, on December 14, 1923, Regina Blumer brought a divorce action on cruelty grounds against Dr. Louis Blumer, who no longer had a medical license. She sought alimony and the custody of their five children. She attached $40,000 worth of her husband's property.

These scandalous events and the subsequent trial were covered in newspapers nationwide for several months, until the spring of 1924."

My mother, Jeanette Rose Blumer, was born in 1908, which would have made her 15 at the time of this disaster. Her mother had, by that time, become a Dr. of Naturopathy herself.

What I was told as a child was that Louis had a relationship with another women and that he even had "another family". That would be a good reason for Regina not to "stand by her man".

Regina and Jeanette never said a word about the other parts of the scandal to us. All they ever said was that he had been unfaithful and had another family. The family's lips were sealed about the charges of fraud and the divorce. They basically decided not to talk about Louis and tried to "disappear" him from their lives.

What difference does all this make today? On the surface it is just an amusing bit of "ancient history", but that is the thing about history, it doesn't just melt away, it is always present in some way. Traumatic history changes the present and keeps making history.

When I was trying to make sense of the puzzle of my life as a troubled adolescent and beyond, I was missing some very important pieces.

Chapter Two

Joy to The World

I have happy memories of my mother, young and joyous, playing with me.

In winter, she liked warm peaked hats with earflaps and ties. I still have one in my closet for digging-the-car-out-of-snow days.

She was lucky to be able to stay home with me in the wake of the Great Depression. She taught me all the little crafty things that I made a living teaching to other little kids much, much later.

I always had the nicest clothes. My father, Aaron Arthur Robins, known as "Robby"', was in the infant and children's clothing business. He was a Resident Buyer, a profession that no longer exists. Small specialty shops in small towns all over the country (which also no longer exist) relied on him to select the clothing they sold, since he was in New York City and they could only rarely get here.

My nana, Regina came to this country alone when she was sixteen. She was the oldest daughter of a middle class Jewish family in Dorahoi Romania. Her father, Jacob Goldstein, a chemist in a brewery, died, leaving only daughters. Their mother, Clara Goldstein, sent her eldest here as a scout.

Regina was welcomed by the family of her hometown barrel makers, the Blumers, who had settled in Middletown Connecticut. Eventually, Regina helped bring her own family here.

We guessed that my great grandfather's name was Jacob. Regina's eldest son was probably named after him.

In the late 19th century, young women from "good families" were expected to be "genteel" and were only taught appropriate occupations, like playing piano and needlework. It was a good thing Regina could sew, because that got her a job in a "sweat shop" in New York.

The garment trade in New York, at the turn of the 20th century was largely Jewish, and that helped. Those were the early days when unions were just getting started, with a lot of help from Jewish garment workers. Regina was already a mother and settled in Hartford Connecticut by the time of the 1911 Triangle Shirtwaist fire which seared sweatshop conditions into our country's memory.

As a "refined" young lady and eventually old lady, Regina always dressed well and kept up the middle class standards of her upbringing, including being careful not to reflect badly on the Jews in general.

Regina was eager to leave old country ways behind. She learned English so well that she had only a slight, almost imperceptible accent.

Part of being "refined" was, unfortunately, an attitude of superiority. I adored my nana when I was a child and I love her still, but she was a racist, like most of her contemporaries.

She gave a lot of thought to religion, one of the things I shared with her when we lived close. She never gave up Judaism, but she subscribed to Unity, a publication of the Unitarian Church. When it became the Unitarian/Universalists, she drew the line. She didn't like being in a group with black people.

Ancestry.com has given us a new perspective on my grandfather, Louis Blumer. He was born in the same small city in Romania, and probably knew Regina when they were both children.

As a young man, he was, as we might say today, “drop dead gorgeous”. By the time he won Regina’s hand, he had become an educated man, a doctor, and a pioneer in an exciting, revolutionary branch of medicine.

Naturopathy was not a bunch of quackery, as the American Medical Association, the strong lobbying arm of the traditional medical practitioners of the day, would have had the public believe. It was, and is, a form of what we now call “holistic medicine”.

The fact that Louis had a noticeable accent was a source of embarrassment for his eldest daughter Jeanette, my mother. She later had much more cause to be embarrassed and ashamed of her father.

I don’t think that the estrangement, the cutting him off, happened early enough that Jeanette didn’t learn a lot from her father. She did take after him. Her older brother and her sisters were blond, taking after the “strawberry blond” Regina. Jeanette was a brunette. The baby, Alvin also had dark hair. He too was "drop dead gorgeous" as a man.

One of the things Louis listed as being taught at The Blumer College of Naturopathy was "Suggestive therapy". He also claimed to be a Doctor of Psychology. Much of the wisdom that my mother passed on to me must have come from her father's grasp of the power of suggestion and psychology.

I used to say my mom was like Sancho Panza, Don Quixote's faithful traveling companion. Sancho was full of little sayings, what we might call now, "bumper sticker" mottos. My mother was also full of them.

I learned to "Live with Courage", and that "Every day in every way I will get better and better", and a whole lot more. I found myself relying on them in my own life and sharing them with my clients when I briefly practiced Family Therapy and when I worked as a Preventative Services Social Worker.

One other thing that was probably an inheritance from Louis Blumer was the "Ungrateful Wretch" speech. I never heard my nana use it but my mother did and when I became a mother I did too. It must have been wide spread in the Jewish Mother culture of the time. My husband, Ralph says that his mother used it too.

(Gertrude) Joy Robins: That's me! I never used the Gertrude, although I considered it an honor. I was named after my father's oldest sister who died trying to have a second child against medical advice. She had had Rheumatic Fever as a child and it had left her with a weak heart. She had been, reportedly, the brightest one of the six siblings. I guess she wanted that baby so much that she risked her life and sadly, lost it.

My father was the one who came up with my middle name "Joy". He remembered that "a thing of beauty is a joy forever". I was definitely welcome, and I always knew it.

I was born in 1936. The United States got into World War II on December 8, 1941.My sister Lorna is 4 years and 10 months younger than me. She was born in May, 1941 and soon there was a war on. The long gap between us is probably a reflection of the uncertainty of the times.

Lorna was always at a disadvantage. No wonder she resented me. She hated that I was her "second mother", and in more than one way I probably tried to be. She was an infant and I was a bright, active five year old. Of course I felt maternal towards her. What else could I do with her?

I was brought home from Women's Hospital in Manhattan to a lovely little house in Jamaica, Queens. It was not the tough neighborhood or the fancy Jamaica Estates that people think of now. It was a middle class suburb with no direct connection to Manhattan. Eventually the subway reached out to it.

I remember that we sold the house and my mom was rewarded with a fur coat, a Persian lamb, for having gotten us such a good price. I never did figure out why we sold the house. Maybe it was too small for the growing family. After that we rented.

As I got older, Jeanette was no longer so joyous about her role. I remember disagreeing strongly with some of her parenting. I was very articulate and unafraid to speak my mind. I still am. I got into a lot of trouble with it then, even more as I got older.

My father believed what he had been taught. His job was not parenting, it was bread-winning and he was not supposed to interfere with my mother's domain. He stood behind my mother and never was a refuge from her, which I could have used.

My only refuge was my nana. From the time we left the house in Jamaica until I was 11, she lived near us in a garden apartment complex set around a closed circle in Kew Gardens, Queens. (Now, I live with my second husband in a co-op garden apartment in a similar circle in Staten Island. I have wondered at the coincidence.)

We moved from the Kew Gardens apartment so that I could go to the new Stephen Halsey Junior High in Forest Hills. There I was in onc of the first of what were known as Special Progress or SP classes.

I did three years in two and stayed with the same wonderful teacher, Miss Tanzee and the same group of children. It was great while it lasted.

Lorna got sick soon after we moved to Forest Hills. My mother was distraught and distracted. She was afraid that Lorna would become deaf or even die. This was not necessarily an over-reaction. In 1946 the most effective antibiotics were Sulfa drugs. In 1947 Penicillin finally started to become available to civilians.

I guess my parents thought they were protecting me by trying to keep what was going on a secret. On my end, it felt like rejection.

In addition, I was on the cusp of adolescence and my father didn't want to cuddle with me anymore. That felt like rejection too.

For six year old Lorna, I think this illness was traumatic and life-changing .She was undoubtedly scared. My mother's anxiety was catching. I think Jeanette evolved from overprotective to controlling at that point. She forged an unhealthy bond with Lorna, confiding in her and defending her inappropriately.

She apparently thought I was doing just fine and needed less attention than I actually did.

I was traumatized too. I had left my nana, my emotional anchor and shield behind in Kew Gardens. I did have Miss Tanzee and my class buddies and was very happy at school, but at home things were rough.

Miss Tanzee must have picked up on that and spoken to my parents about getting me some help. I remember my mom taking me around to doctors and getting me hormone tests. Surprise, doesn't every girl on the cusp of puberty have a hormone imbalance?

Lorna recovered from the illness eventually, with just some hearing loss in one ear. I don't think she has ever recovered emotionally.

When he became a commercial artist, I think my Uncle Jack may have spelled it Blummer to sound more gentile. My Uncle Alvin later changed it to Plummer to go all the way. My mother used to say she was Episcopalian for the same reason, to get work.

There was a lot of prejudice against Jews in those days. I pretty much escaped it, not because it was over when I was a kid, but because I grew up in Queens Neighborhoods where pretty much everyone else was Jewish.

My father's family were not secular Romanians. They were from Russia. I picture them in a "schetal", a small town in the Pale, as in "Fiddler on the Roof".

My father's mother was called Lena. I think she died before my sister was born. My sister gave the impression at my father's funeral that Lena was alive when she was born, but Jews name after the honored dead. She had to have been named after her.

My father always honored his mother, and my mother looked down her nose at her. She never really learned English, she didn't accept the "dress code", and she had that dreadful disease, poverty; at least until her children grew up and were able to support her in a style to which she had not been accustomed. When I was little, Lena used to show her love by knitting me wonderful warm gloves. I remember when she became "senile". It got me very upset that I was no longer allowed to talk to her.

I was Lena's first granddaughter. My Aunt Rose, with whom she lived in the Bronx, had given her two grandsons; Harry and Jerry Mandel. Her oldest daughter Gertrude, after whom I was named, had given her one grandson, Sanford Lakeoff, "Sandy".

My boy cousins were a great gift to me and I had a wonderful time with them as a child.

I loved my Uncle Herman and Aunt Connie Robins who lived in Norfolk Virginia. They laughed a lot and always did a lively hora duo at weddings and bar mitzvahs.

My mother did not approve of my father's brothers. He loosened up too much with them at those family events and, God forbid, drank enough to get drunk.

I remember the fights when she called him a "shicker" (drunk). Nothing could be further from the truth. He enjoyed a scotch or two until he died, but he never got drunk as far as I know, without his brothers.

My mother looked down her nose at Aunt Connie, but she was spunky and reciprocated by considering Jeanette a snob.

The name Robins came from Rabinowitz, and translates "son of rabbis". My grandfather, "Captain Mike", chose the one b and the s. Other members of the family went with other spellings.

My granduncles, Harry and Ben Robin, started "Robin's Confectionary" in Norfolk Virginia. It was a modest success at first and occasioned a call for some of my uncles to go down there and help out.

The oldest, my Uncle Julie, went first and later, my Uncle Herman ("Robby II") left his position with the New York City Police Force and followed. He took his gun and kept it under the counter for protection. The neighborhood was getting rougher.

We would go down to Norfolk to visit on the way to Florida, during the winter vacation from school, which coincided with the slack season in the garment trade.

We would also go down for family occasions such as the bar mitzvahs and weddings of my cousins.

Over the years, my Uncle Julie and his wife Etta invited us to my oldest cousin, Muriel's wedding and Cousin Buddy's bar mitzvah and wedding. His name was really Arnold. They were much older than my sister and me.

Herman and Connie had two daughters, Harriet and Mickey, whose real name was Marion, after Captain Mike, I think. They were younger than me and I never really got close to them. Lorna kept in touch.

My Granduncle Ben became disabled with Muscular Dystrophy. His younger brother Harry stayed with him and took care of him. He would lift him and bathe him, sacrificing any other life that might have been there for him. He was the first hero that I knew personally. He died of a heart attack before Ben died.

Ben had a devoted live-in Aide after Harry died. He was a black man, but he too was a hero, at least to Ben.

My father's youngest brother was also called Ben. He married a woman older than himself and with an accent. They had one son. They lived on Long Island, which was much closer to us, but we saw very little of them.

Chapter Three

Moving On

My mother, as the oldest daughter, had long had a lot of duties laid on her. She grew up keeping the books for the Blumer College of Naturopathy and helped care for her younger sisters and brother. Her older brother Jack worked in the Blumer College print shop. His father reportedly beat him; an acceptable recourse in those days. I don't know if Louis beat his wife too.

Regina was probably too much for her husband to handle, with the independence she had gained in the new world and her ideas about women's equality.

She had worked before they married and served as the Secretary of the Blumer College of Naturopathy. There she also gained a profession, along with the five children. Her working was in aid of the family business, which was acceptable, but it later enabled her to leave her husband.

When her mother left her father, Jeanette was the one with the "business head." Her mother leaned on her. Regina worked as a Naturopathist for a while and was awarded a settlement in the divorce. Still, the Depression hit and times were tough.

Regina eventually settled in Brooklyn. As the children got older they all had to pitch in. Jeanette worked as a bookkeeper. She said she just kept learning on the job and lost a few jobs in the process.

She met my father in New York. They were married in 1932. Both were lucky enough to have jobs. They worked hard and saved to put a down payment on a little house in Queens.

When I came, four years later, Jeanette was a lucky stay- at- home mom. Although that was the cultural ideal, in the wake of the Depression it was more of a privilege for her and a blessing for me.

Aaron, better known as Robby, never finished High School. He had found work in the garment district. He then went into business with a partner as Robins and Lowenstein Resident Buyers. Lowenstein eventually died but Robby kept him on the letterhead.

When Lorna went to school and Jeanette could work, she typed the letters, kept the books and mimeographed the newsletters that were sent to Robins and Lowenstein clients.

Regina struggled for many years. Naturopathy was not recognized in New Jersey or New York. She ended up as an Industrial Nurse with American Safety Razor in Brooklyn. She retired with a small pension and late in life used some of her money to help Adeline and her husband, Jack Levin, build a house with a dental office in it in Dumont, New Jersey.

In exchange, they built a little apartment upstairs in which Regina lived happily until she died.

"Brother Jack" eventually married a gentile, “Dolly” who was red headed and “pleasantly plump” like his mother. They had three children, my cousins; Jonny, Clara Jean and Hannah. Hannah is the only one still alive today. Her sister died young. She had juvenile diabetes, what they call “type one” today.

Hannah ended up marrying her sister’s widower. That seems to have worked out well and has lasted over 20 years so far.

Jonny, the eldest, also died young and was reportedly married twice. I remember the first marriage was with an older woman who already had children. He gave her another. He had other children with the second wife and was reputedly abusive with them, as his father had been with him.

We lost touch with Dolly and her children when Jack died. Regina had never approved of her and she apparently reciprocated.

Jacob Blumer AKA Jon L. Blummer died at only 51. I was at his funeral. Regina was distraught and had allowed Alvin to make the arrangements. He negotiated with Dolly who was still Christian and with the clergyman who was to conduct the service. It ended up that he must have misunderstood what Alvin meant. He did a nondenominational Christian service instead of one suitable for a Jew. He said that the way to heaven was through Jesus Christ. My nana was so angry and upset that she couldn't properly mourn her son until later.

The middle sister, Gertrude married a gentile engineer, Walter Gregory. They never had children, I think because it was a "mixed marriage". In those days there were a lot of concerns about what religion to raise the children in. Of course, as the child of a "messy" divorce, Gertrude might not have wanted children.

Adeline, the youngest, was the prettiest of the Blumer girls and had to be talked out of trying a career in show business. Regina had known Sophie Tucker and thought she was far less than genteel. Adeline then scored a dentist. The only thing better in the Jewish Mother ranking was a doctor.

Jack Levin adored Adeline and was the model for what to look for in a husband for me and my daughters in later years.

Alvin, the youngest, continued to live with Regina until he went into the Army Air Corps in WWII.

When he came back he married Jane who was a neurotic Manhattanite. She didn't want children because she knew she would not be able to be a proper mother. She was Alvin's childlike bride and he took good care of her until she died.

Late in life he met his "soul mate", a gentile woman called Louise. They had too few years together but they were very good years. They are buried together in Utah.

My theory is that women pick either the positive or negative image of their fathers. Like the positive or negative of a photograph. I picked a man unlike my father. I think all three of the Blumer sisters did that too.

Men tend to be like their fathers and learn to father from them. They tend to pick women like their mothers.

Women learn to mother from their mothers and if they get too little "mothering" meaning unconditional love, they have difficulty giving it themselves.

Chapter Four

Keeping Score

I thought of my parents as "the gingham dog and the calico cat" from the poem, "The Duel" by Eugene Field. "The truth about the cat and pup is this: they ate each other up!"

They clearly loved each other but there was little harmony in their day-to-day interactions while I was growing up. One thing was clear, they were evenly matched.

That would seem, on the surface, to be the case with Louis and Regina Blumer as well.

This is the account of Phil Gold, a relative who completed a family history in 1997, shortly before he died in his nineties.

"Uncle Louis was the first one in the family to own an automobile. He had a REO touring car and drove it with a wild abandon. Louis was a progressive type, wore colorful clothes; the first man I saw wear knickers. Regina, with her red hair, was a fiery type of person. She was very bright, quick to anger, more with her family than with others. Their life style in retrospect was what I used to think as rather affluent.

Louis and Regina were divorced in the 1920s, but as I learned much later it was a quite messy one, which was not a surprise to me, knowing the temperament of both parties. The action cost Louis Blumer everything he had; cash, property and the children...."

It would appear that in the Blumer divorce, the blame and the consequences were apportioned equally.

People seem to want to have it that way, it is very convenient, but in a world where the man has most of the advantages, it usually isn't.

It took some time but we were able to get a copy of the actual divorce papers.

No allegations were made about another woman at all, but the charges of cruelty were well documented.

"(a) Sometime during the spring of the year 1920,..the defendant attacked the plaintiff in her bedroom...struck her and beat her and felled her to the floor, and tore off part of her clothes and ordered her to leave the house.

(b) At various times during the year 1921 the defendant cruelly beat and bruised the minor children of the plaintiff with an instrument of punishment fashioned by the defendant for this purpose, said instrument being known as a cat-o'-nine-tails made of leather; and on one occasion when the plaintiff protested the defendant's acts, the defendant turned upon the plaintiff and struck her repeatedly upon her body with said instrument.

(c)During the year 1922 at various times the defendant struck and beat the plaintiff and threatened to kill her, and displayed a revolver which he threatened to use to kill

the plaintiff and to kill the plaintiff's and defendant's minor children.

(d)At various times since 1920 the defendant has accused the plaintiff of trying to poison him by administering poison in his food, and repeatedly the defendant has compelled one of the minor children, in the presence of the plaintiff, to partake of food prepared for the defendant by the plaintiff, meantime accusing the plaintiff of an intent to poison the defendant.

(e)At numerous times when the defendant has inflicted cruelties upon the plaintiff as hereinbefore set forth the defendant has cursed the plaintiff in vile, profane, obscene and blasphemous language in the presence of the children of the plaintiff and defendant, and in the presence of other persons, and has applied to the plaintiff low and vile and obscene epithets.

(f)At various times over a period of years, prior to 1923, the defendant has cruelly beaten and bruised and otherwise maltreated the minor children of the plaintiff and defendant, against the protests of the plaintiff.

As a result of said acts of the defendant toward the plaintiff, the plaintiff stands in great fear of the defendant for her safety of life and limb and for the safety of said minor children."

Well, it appears that my grandfather was a full-fledged abuser! No wonder Regina waited until the Sheriff took him away to leave and to file for divorce! Guys like that still regularly kill their spouses for having the nerve to leave them. That might also explain why Regina was so careful about who knew where to find her.

It is clear that my mother and her siblings were traumatized by these events and that fueled the secrecy defense. Secrecy is isolating. It is getting stuck in denial and that can be very damaging psychologically.

The divorce papers also show that while Regina was awarded a sizable settlement, she probably did not receive most of it. Louis claimed that he was now unemployed and the property, now no longer a college, was not worth anywhere near as much as it had been.

Phil Gold continued: *"After the divorce, Louis edited and published a health magazine from his 3 room office suite on*

Main, corner Sheldon St. He also utilized the practice of clientele he had built up in previous years....Louis at long last, retired to Florida, had a small practice and survived poorly....

I have a copy of Louis' obituary notice from the "Miami Herald" dated April 2, 1959. It was headlined "Naturopathy Founder dies at 78".

Actually Louis was not the founder of Naturopathy, but he was a pioneer in its practice.

While he did not exactly prosper, he did not support his five children either.

Again, no mention is made of another woman. That was probably the cover story that the family adopted. It would be believable and much less painful than the truth. If he had a girlfriend during or after the marriage, wouldn't Phil have mentioned it? It would have been perfectly respectable after the divorce.

Chapter Five

Falling Apart and Coming Together

Lorna had a double whammy as a very young child. First she got sick and had the bejeebers scared out of her, and then I got sick and was exiled to a mental hospital, leaving her alone with dysfunctional parents.

"Mental Illness" is a politically correct term and reflects our more progressive efforts to understand those afflicted and include them in the human family. In the late forties and early fifties these niceties were not observed. I went "crazy" and was put in the "nut house" or more accurately the "snake pit".

I don't remember too much about that time, probably because they gave me shock treatments. Later, I got very little information out of my mother, in spite of my long-term concerted effort to find out what had happened. She was obviously ashamed and felt the best thing was to suppress any effort to remember and move on. I have moved on, but at that time, I needed very much to deal with what had precipitated my break with reality and she was no help. She did communicate the shame, and that has been a burden and a barrier, until now.

What I know is that my parents had left my sister and me with my nana while they went on a vacation trip to California. It was a reward for Jeanette's having pulled Lorna through her illness.

I must have acted up enough for my nana to call them and tell them she couldn't handle me. They came home early and I was taken away by men in white coats, kicking and screaming: "I hate my mother! I hate my father! Why can't I just live with my nana and my sister?"

Eventually, my parents broke open my college fund piggy bank and had me transferred from Belleview to a nice place on Long Island. There were cottages with other kids and "house mothers", a bowling alley and arts and crafts.

I saw a Psychologist occasionally and was enrolled in a Correspondence School. I still didn't want to see my parents, which is probably why they still thought I was crazy.

I finally asked the Psychologist why other kids, who had been there a shorter time and hadn't seemed to be doing any better than me, had gone home and I was still there. He said I didn't want to go home. That was the truth.

I decided to work my way out of there. The first thing was to let my parents visit. They brought Lorna. I remember how scared she looked, with big eyes like a fawn in the headlights.

I decided I really needed to go home to help her. She was alone with them. I had apparently been a buffer and had partially protected her while I was there.

I was always interested in what made people tick. I later learned a lot about psychology both in college and in my efforts to help my daughters.

I took a course in Family Therapy and even practiced it for a short time. It is true that in a dysfunctional family there is often a "weak link" who is the first to show symptoms, and it is usually a child.

I was a victim, and like the victims of rape or incest, I was not guilty of bringing on the trauma.

Chapter Six

There Goes The Bride.

While I still loved my parents, I no longer trusted them. I was always watching my back lest they try to drop the butterfly net over me again. I determined to keep a low profile until I was finally 21 and legally out of their control.

I can’t say I didn’t have any fun along the way, even carrying the shameful unanswered questions in my own little Pandora’s Box.

While I was In Leonia High School I had my first real boyfriend and went to the prom. I graduated and went on to college. The college fund having been blown, I went to Fairleigh Dickenson in nearby Teaneck, commuting by bus the first year.

I wanted to avoid the horror that was Bergen County public transportation in my second year, so I got a job at a department store in Hackensack and saved up money to buy a car. The summer before my sophomore year, my father helped me find a reliable car at the Chevy dealership. He didn't want me driving a piece of junk.

While I had a good down payment already; to get that car, I needed to finance a small amount. Still being a minor, I needed a cosigner. While I shouldn't have been surprised, I was very hurt that even though he was not being asked to lay out a cent, my father gave me a hard time about signing that paper. He eventually relented, but my slowly-being-rebuilt ego took a hit that would not be forgotten.

My father made a good faith effort to teach me to drive that little Chevy. It wasn't easy because the back of the passenger seat kind of flopped back. Also, my father was prone to high blood pressure and it looked like it might kill him.

I took lessons at a driving school and finally, at 19, got my license. The little Chevy kept running well after I graduated college. My sister drove it awhile. I remember it being parked, still in running condition, in the back of the little infants' and children's shop that my parents ended up in when the resident buying business died. They had already moved to Oradell by way of Teaneck and I had been married for some time.

At the end of my junior year, I heard about a college-run tour of Europe that sounded good and was reasonably priced. I was thinking of it for the end of my senior year, which would give me enough time to earn the money. To my astonishment, my parents offered to pay for the tour so that I could go that summer. That was the summer I was to turn 21.

I hesitated but figured, "what could possibly go wrong?" Plenty! It was the first time I was out of that house and on my own since I had returned from the "funny farm". I started to peek into my Pandora's Box and try to figure out the answers to the awful questions: What had happened that led me to be committed? What part had my parents played? Was it my fault? Was I fatally flawed? Was it genetic? I started to drive myself crazy!

Luckily, I was able to stuff the demons back into the box and get it closed again. Unfortunately, there was a price. Because I had acted "unstable", they sent me home early and the college, while letting me graduate, withheld the teaching certification that was supposed to be part of completing the Early Childhood Education curriculum.

By the time I got home from that trip, I had righted myself, was convincingly sane; and soon crossed to the safety of legal majority. I had too little ego strength left to go for the road less traveled: graduate college, get a job, save money and move out. So, I started looking in earnest for my Prince Charming.

My parents had made it clear that they would only pay for education if it was a ticket to a job, but even though "Fairleigh Ridiculous" as we used to call it, was no Ivy League school, I did get an education.

By my senior year I had taken all the requirements for the Early Childhood Education major. The Ed courses were awful. They were all about "methods" and not about content. We, who had not done Geography since we ourselves had been in grade school, were being taught how to teach it, with no update at all about what it entailed; this, in the age of the UN, in which the number of countries on the map had been increasing exponentially.

I was finally free to take courses I didn't have to take. I accumulated enough credits for at least a couple of more majors and a few minors. I took Psychology, English and History. My Biology teacher was great, but I was fascinated with my American History teacher, Margaret L. Coit, who had written what is still the definitive biography of John C. Calhoun. She was kooky, smart and super interesting, the only actual author I had ever met.

While FDU was a commuter school and had very little campus life, we did hang out in the cafeteria and occasionally meet people that were not in our classes. I had one very attractive male friend. He never asked me out, but was sincerely interested in what I thought. It later dawned on me that he was what we now call Gay. Another male friend was a photographer and eventually did the pictures of my wedding.

I had girlfriends. All but one served at my wedding; three as bridesmaids and one playing the piano. The exception was really my best friend, Joyce Martin. She was a little older because she had had Polio and spent more than a year in a cast. Her back was a little crooked still, but she was not crippled. I asked my parents if I could invite her over for dinner. I was stunned when they said "absolutely not!" Of course I should have known; she was what we used to call a "Negro". (What would the neighbors think?) That didn't stop me from asking her to be in my wedding. She told me that she couldn't because her childhood best friend was being married the same day. I think now that she understood my family's attitudes better than I did.

I had been doing my homework. I met Zelik at a Jewish Singles event. He could be charming, but he was certainly no prince.

I was a virgin at 21 and horny as hell. I had been dating, but up to then, no one who was a serious candidate had come along.

Zelik was horny too. He was an experienced "older man" in my mind. He was a year older than me and had been married briefly before. It had been annulled. He had been in the army, but was discharged with a "bad back" and was receiving a small disability check monthly. He was working at his father's bakery and had the promise of a partnership.

Zelik relieved me of my virginity on the wicker sofa with leather cushions in the enclosed side porch of the house on Oakdene Avenue in Leonia, NJ. My parents and sister were upstairs.

I didn't know much about sex that I hadn't learned from Margaret Mead, but my mother had taught me about contraception.

Zelik didn't bring "protection" that first time. He didn't like condoms because they took away from his pleasure. He tried to assure me that early withdrawal would be enough to keep me from getting pregnant. I was not convinced and spent some very anxious days waiting for my period. Abortion was illegal and often fatal in those days.

I finally relaxed when I was able to talk my mother into taking me to the gynecologist for a diaphragm. My excuse was that I needed it for my honeymoon. Frank had asked me to marry him. I was convinced that I was in love with him.

He had passed one important test. I had told him that I had been in a mental hospital and he didn't seem to care. He was pretty mixed up emotionally himself and I saw that as a kind of parity.

We were married on June 29, 1958, not long after my college graduation. I turned 22 on July 16. It was a beautiful wedding, planned by me to be tasteful but not too expensive. It was at the temple in nearby Palisades Park.

Rabbi Block was not only a wonderful Rabbi and a mensch, but he took a turn at the drums at the reception which was in the room downstairs.

My dress was borrowed but I was not blue. I really meant the vows I took under the hoopa. I was out of that house at last!

Chapter Seven

Married Life

I remember my first honeymoon now. I hadn't thought of it for a very long time. We went to the Neville, a big and impressive hotel in the Catskills. We were young, and fancier than that was not feasible.

I remember Zelik had to put the mattress on the floor before we could lie down, because of his bad back. I had high hopes for the marriage bed, but alas, he was less than eager. We didn't do it until the next morning and he was not interested in sticking around the room after that, with all that tennis available.

I found myself in the hotel library, holding back tears and wondering what I had gotten myself into.

When we got back to our little garden apartment in Fairlawn, I put all that out of my mind and started getting organized.

I soon began to enjoy being a young married woman. I was decorating a home for the first time and was a pretty good cook. I wasn't expected to work. Zelik brought in enough money. His father's bakery was nearby.

I was able to make a home for both of us, and not too long afterward, for our first baby, my sunny little honey, "Gigi".

My nana, who died not long after I was married, had made me promise that I would wait two years before having children. (That was an important lesson she had taken from her own life.) Well, I almost made it. I was married June 29, 1958. Regina Ruth Shulman was born May 30, 1960.

I used to joke that having three children in three and a half years was like spending "seven years with my head in the toilet" (a reference to rinsing cloth diapers); but I had never been happier. Zelik brought in enough money and I could stay home and concentrate on what I later dubbed my first preschool class.

Zelik had wanted a family too, and was attentive when I was pregnant, although he never helped with the above mentioned dirty diapers or any of the housework. I was used to that division of labor from my parents' model of marriage and accepted it.

Having taken for granted the Boy Scout aspects of my father, I had chosen a man who was more "intellectual", and exciting. Little did I know how exciting.

Zelik did not have friends; he had family, lots of it. While his mother, Edna Sophie, had only one sister, Mary, his father, Israel, AKA "Solik", later known as Charlie, had so many brothers I lost count. Zelik was an only child. His youngest uncle, Ruben, was his best man.

As I learned to love him, Zelik used to confide in me how brutally his father had cut him off at the knees. "Who do you think you are? You think you are better than anyone else?" It put poor little Zelik in his place and inspired him never to rise above his father's station. He was very bright but never graduated college and confined himself to success in his father's working class mold. He ran the bakery's stable of sales clerks and later managed his own bakery.

Still later he ran a lunch truck; and then a few lunch trucks, etc. He made lots of money, but he could not “succeed”.

When Zelik finally found a calling and aspired to be an actor, he just couldn’t follow through. He couldn’t handle the rejection of auditions and just stopped trying.

Chapter Eight

Reflections

As a student of Child Development, I know it matters when someone is traumatized. Children as they get older develop better defenses.

I took my blow when I was an early adolescent. Lorna took hers while still in early childhood. Zelik took his first and worst, in infancy.

What we are to call trauma matters. I believe it is an event or situation that is perceived as being acutely life threatening.

As a Social Worker, I found Post Traumatic Stress Disorder in a great many of my clients. Since then, it has been confirmed that not only doesn't it take actual shells to cause "shell shock" but PTSD is far too common in civilians, not just in armed forces personnel.

Zelik heard "get rid of the baby" and he was a baby. Lorna really thought she was going to die of that ear infection. I thought I was going to die when they held me down and ran electricity through my brain. (At least now they use anesthesia.)I believe that I was "emotionally disturbed" to begin with, but became traumatized by the "treatment" I received.

Emotional support matters a great deal in building resilience. My parents had been doting, if over protective, and I had my nana to validate my intellectual life. I also had the Special Progress, open classroom, model of cooperation and accomplishment. It is not surprising that I was drawn to Early Childhood Education and later helped to start an Alternative School.

Lorna had me as a buffer but I was kept away while she was ill and later sent away; a lesson to her to keep a low profile.

Not surprising that she could not break away from an emotional dependence on my mother and still cannot give unconditional love to her daughter.

I am probably not the first person to notice that the term Narcissism is misleading. It brings to mind the myth of the beautiful young man falling in love with his image in the water.

I think It really has more to do with fear than love. A child who fears for his or her life probably doesn't have much energy left to love. Fear can destroy the trust that children need to grow emotionally.

Zelik needs to keep others off balance and put them down. He battered me emotionally and used his knowledge of my doubts and fears about my own mental health to "Gaslight" me.

I have had almost no firsthand experience with him for many years. I hope he has "mellowed", but I doubt it. I survived our marriage because I was a poor casting choice for Masochist.

I lived through it, and have always thought that what my daughters suffered was Post Traumatic Stress Disorder, in the wake of the train wreck that was our divorce.

All three of them fell apart differently, yet the powers-that-be slapped the same diagnosis on all of them.

I thought "Manic Depression", now called "Bipolar Disorder" was the "diagnosis of the month". It seems to have had far more staying power than that, but it is still bull sh**t.

Traumatic history changes the present and keeps making history. Slavery and the horrendous blood bath that finally ended it in the United States can still be felt in the lives, not just of people of color, but of all Americans.

At Passover, Jews remember the traumatic events of the Exodus from Egypt. The slavery that the Egyptians visited on the early Hebrews seems almost humane in comparison to American Slavery. The American pre-Civil War South had perfected slavery as an assault on Humanity. The events of the Holocaust dwarf the less organized, although numerous, previous assaults on the Jews.

I think human beings are hardwired for religion. If we don't know why something happens, we make up a reason and it expands. We don't like randomness and try to make order.

As a girl, I gave a lot of thought to the subject of "Is there a God?" and other such weighty questions. I was lucky to have Regina, my nana, to discuss them with.

She was happy to have me drop by. It was during WWII and she was getting letters from her youngest, Alvin, with lots of holes in them from the censors. He was in the Army Air Corps and we found out later that he was doing reconnaissance for the Normandy invasion.

I decided before I was 10 that I was a Deist, like many of the founding fathers. I even sent for a copy of Tom Paine's Common Sense, which came in a plain brown wrapper. (It probably still does.) God had to exist, the universe was the only testament needed for that. The definition of God was the remaining problem. I decided eventually that the Hindus had it right. God could not be made in the image of man; no white beard - a creative, amorphous, all pervasive force. That didn't mean that it wasn't OK to express the attributes of that force in human form or with trees, rocks or what have you.

I think Judaism is a good religion. It is clear that God is one and it does not elevate any human being to godhood. Moses is deliberately not mentioned in the Seder. It was God that brought the people out of Egypt.

There is a lot of wonderful wisdom that is conveyed in the Sabbath service. I picked up much that has stuck, especially since in the Reform Temple it is in English.

I was never bat mitzvoth, nor was my sister, nor were most of the young women of my generation. Judaism is a patriarchal religion and women are definitely considered less valuable than men. That has changed slowly over the years, mostly in the more liberal denominations.

Christianity is an update, or you could even say a "spin-off", of Judaism. Jesus was a Jew and a real historical figure. I believe in him, even though I don't think he had any intention of becoming the man-god that he was made into. If Jesus could have envisioned how he is remembered, I don't think he would have liked it.

However, the Jewish sect that evolved into Christianity did make some of the good parts of Judaism available to the practitioners of religions that were much further from monotheism.

In the beginning of Christianity, the Jewish members of that splinter cult insisted that staying Kosher and strictly adhering to the many demanding strictures of an already very old and well -developed religion was absolutely necessary. That view did not win out in the end. That left this branch of Judaism open to many more converts than any other monotheistic religion available. It was about time for this very logical idea to take off.

Far in the past, the Egyptian Pharaoh, Akhenaton, had "seen the light" of Monotheism. This was well before the Hebrews left Egypt and it is very likely that they got the idea from him.

As Pharaoh, He had the power to introduce his new religion of one God, symbolized by Aton, the sun. He moved his capital and built a great city from scratch, to honor this unitary deity.

Unfortunately, the time was not right and in spite of his god-king status as Pharaoh, his efforts were eventually defeated. After his death, his city was destroyed and abandoned.

His son, Tutankhamen, the boy-king famous for his undisturbed treasures, had been originally named Tutankhaton in honor of the One God. The priests of the other ancient gods had their way with him and with Egypt.

Christianity was more flexible than Judaism at the time it was developing. Many elements of the indigenous faiths of the people that converted ended up in Christianity. In the end, that was inevitable and probably a good thing.

Chapter Nine

Detour

We were only in the little apartment in Fairlawn for a very short time. Our discussions about the situation with his dad had led Zelik to want to break free. He found an opportunity on Long Island and we took an apartment in Ronkonkoma.

Gigi was only about nine months old, crawling from room to room with glee. Zelik was selling freezer plans.

Edna Sophie couldn't stand the separation from her beloved granddaughter a second longer. It was the middle of winter but she wanted to come and stay with us, just for a few days. We didn't have much choice. She came and we set her up in the living room on the couch.

Then it snowed, and snowed and snowed. We were snowed in. The roads were bad, the trains weren't running. We had enough food for awhile, but when we went to bed, Zelik wanted sex and we had no condoms.

I couldn't use the diaphragm yet because I was still recovering from the birth. Everything wasn't back in place. So with my mother-in-law in the next room, we took our chances.

I wanted more children anyway, so it was actually fortunate that I conceived. My second daughter, Holly Sue joined us in my womb that night in the crowded little apartment. I think her Hebrew name is Hannah Sarah, after one of her father's grandmothers. I always felt it was for my Granduncle Harry.

I would have gone back to having a tipped uterus and it would have been hard for me to conceive, as it had been with my first, if it had not been for the snow and Edna Sophie.

Shortly after, Zelik gave up his bid for independence. The Freezer Plan business wasn't going well and we were feeling economic pressure. Not only that, we were expecting another child.

Zelik went to his parents and got an offer he couldn't refuse, a partnership in the very profitable bakery business in Fairlawn, known as Rambach's.

By the time our third daughter, Miriam Beth came, we were in our lovely ranch house in Glen Rock. She was also named after a Shulman grandmother, but for me it was for Captain Mike.

The house was perfect. It had a little pool in the back yard that was supposed to be decorative, but it was just deep enough for my toddlers to splash in. It had a jalousied porch in the back that made a large sunny play room for the kids with plenty of storage space for toys.

Glen Rock had a great municipal pool. The children splashed in the kiddy pool while the mothers chatted. I made friends and was very happy for a while.

I joined the League of Women Voters and had the meetings at my house, so I didn't need a baby sitter. I got to use the lovely china and silverware I had been given as wedding gifts.

At first, Zelik would bring home so much baked goods that I was getting really fat. I had put on weight after every birth and my weight was still going up.

My mom and I went to Weight Watchers together. At that time it was a very new program. It worked! I lost weight and was able to march proudly in a parade with the League of Women Voters dressed as a flapper.

Later, I worked for Weight Watchers as a Lecturer, helping others as I had been helped. It was a great experience.

In Glen Rock I made a friend that lived in the neighborhood named Kathy. I think she had a total of four young children. Kathy and I really got along. Then tragedy struck. Her oldest daughter Susan became very ill.

I helped out by watching the younger children while she went around from doctor to doctor trying to find out what was wrong. She finally found out that Susan had a brain tumor. She had already lost some sight and needed an operation or she would die. There was no telling how much of her faculties she would be able to recover.

While Kathy was going through this ordeal, I was able to watch what was happening in her home. She never complained, but her husband did virtually nothing to help, even though Kathy had already been stretched to the limit before Susan became so desperately ill. He went to work and came home and expected dinner to be ready

I was familiar with the “old rules” from my father’s attitude when I was growing up. Men didn’t cook, clean or take care of children. That was demeaning and unbecoming of their masculinity.

It was the early sixties. I think I had already read Betty Freidan’s book, The Feminine Mystique. It began to occur to me that my husband wasn’t any better than Kathy’s.

I think Kathy's husband began to see me as a bad influence and told Kathy to cut me off. In any case, she did.

Much later, I ran into her at a street fair. I was there for the "No Nukes" demonstration; she was there for something else. She said she was still married and that Susan had recovered significantly and was in college.

I had three very small children, a house to take care of, laundry to do and meals to make and shop for. We had cats and I changed the litter box. On top of that, my husband brought home a puppy and expected me to train it and take care of it. The children were too little to help and the active dog, while still small, would just knock them over. I finally put my foot down and the dog was given away. I had it trained by then so that part was easy.

Zelik went out in the evenings whenever he wanted to but rarely took care of the children so I could go out. I began to feel as though I was married and he wasn't. I used to joke that he wasn't a parent, he was "Monstro", the kitten who was so much bigger than the others in the litter that he always got top tit.

I eventually realized that was pretty much the case. I think Zelik picked a mother for himself as well as for his children. I had picked a man more exciting than my dad and instead got an overgrown son. His father's example began to assert itself. He would stay out all night and say he was playing bridge. I would lie in bed and cry and yell at him when he did get home.

I had picked Zelik because he wanted children and seemed like he would be a good father and a good provider. I assumed that he would be a good husband. Well one out of three is all I got. We had all the food we could eat and a nice house, but I was increasingly miserable.

I eventually made the case to Zelik that I needed help. He never considered pitching in himself, but he suggested that we take in his teenaged cousin,

Iris, who had been having trouble at home and had been placed in a group setting. That was then about to close. Iris didn't want to go home and her parents didn't want her to either. I had my doubts that a troubled teen would be much help but Zelik insisted.

Iris tried, but I was right, she was more of a "caseload" than a help. We paid for her to see a therapist, and eventually he suggested that she be allowed to have a dog.

That was it for me. I said "no" loud and clear. By this time I had learned just who would be taking care of that dog and I was just not going to allow it.

Iris went home and somehow made it through. She married and had twin boys. She sadly, died young.

Zelik came up with another solution that didn't involve him helping in the house. He hired a live in maid. She turned out to be a caseload and a half. Actually, I was working with her in an attempt to help her cope so that she could actually function. She was an alcoholic and my efforts were in vain.

Chapter Ten

The Sounds of Silence

My niece got in touch with me after a long silence, in 2011. She had been through the mill with her mother, my sister Lorna. She had almost died and Lorna had turned her back on her.

Melody had been on her own for a long time and while it was an unconventional business, she had been in business successfully.

She was living in Portland Oregon, a very "groovy" place after graduating from Evergreen College and metamorphosing into Isis.

I had visited her at College. It was a very "new age" place and she was really in her element there.

From what I could understand from her website “Waking the Seed”, she was espousing an accepting attitude towards sex and directing her message primarily at women who had been repressing their feelings and their sexuality.

She seemed to be in the right place at the right time in Portland and was being taken seriously and not with a leer. Then times changed. There was a major Recession and there apparently wasn’t enough money loose in her clientele’s jeans to pay for her classes and courses.

She was offering an online course, “podcast” as opposed to broadcast. I was interested in it and I wanted to help her.

Since my Aunt Adeline kept sending me money in the dark days of my divorce, I have been in the habit of sending $100 checks to my daughters, in her name, when they seemed to need it. I extended my circle to include Isis and signed up my long dead Aunt for her course.

Well, my thirty-something niece, who calls herself an “Empath”, turned out to be everything she said she was and more.

With her hypnotic voice and sharp insights, plus her extremely well produced videos with perfectly coordinated sound, she swept me away.

She opened me up and helped me get rid of the shame that had haunted me since I learned from my mother's silence that my illness had been shameful. I finally had someone I could talk to about it and talking about it was what I had always needed to do.

I was ready for Holly's challenge at last, although I don't think Holly was ready then. I don't know if she is yet, but I can't go back to not facing the truth.

I remember the incident she had bad dreams about when she was a preschooler. Her baby sister had gotten into the habit of slipping out of the front door of our Glen Rock ranch house and had been apprehended some distance away, around our suburban block. Luckily, she had not tried to cross the street. Mickey seemed to think it was a lark and I had the challenge of letting her know that she must not do it again.

I set up the pen Holly described using the living room furniture and pillows. I don't think I was yelling, but I was using a firm tone because I wanted

Mickey to know that she was not to do this again and it was dangerous, like touching a hot stove.

At a year and a half, we used to call Mickey, “Screaming Mimi”. We had to stay out of restaurants because she had such good lungs, a piercing tone and determined persistence.

She was applying those skills with a vengeance and it is not surprising that Holly, then three and a half, thought I was hurting her. Holly was also very sensitive to loud noises. As I look back, I see that it may have been traumatic to her. She asked her dad, who had just come home, if he thought I was crazy. He didn't say "no".

That Zelik thought, or at least said he thought, that it was being inappropriate was probably a reflection of his ignorance of early childhood and of parenting in general. It may well have reflected his desire to put me down and be top parent in Holly’s eyes. He succeeded in undermining me as a parent and eroding her trust in me.

He was making me miserable and defining my reactions, such as crying and yelling at him, as “crazy”. Since we moved shortly after the incident described above, it could have been either in Glen Rock or in North Plainfield that he dropped the butterfly net over me and had me taken to a mental hospital.

This time I was well over 21 and completely sane. I was deeply hurt and very angry at Zelik, but I was definitely not crazy. They kept me in only a few days for "observation" and sent me home with the recommendation that I see a counselor.

I had heard a new record in the hospital that reached out to me in my lonely place and comforted me. It was Simon and Garfunkel's "Sounds of Silence".

'"Fools", said I, "You do not know
Silence like a cancer grows
Hear my words that I might teach you
Take my arms that I might reach you"
But my words, like silent raindrops fell
And echoed
In the wells of silence'

By the time I got home, I realized that the marriage wasn't working and I determined to make it work or work my way out of it.

Chapter Eleven

An Offer I Couldn't Refuse

In North Plainfield, Zelik finally left his father behind. He was in a new bakery in nearby Westfield called Margie's Cake Box with his old partner Bill.

We became involved in the development of an Alternative School. Of course we called it Children of the Rainbow School. In college I had learned a lot about the open classroom method of teaching. No desks bolted to the floor with the teacher in the front of the room pontificating. It was a way to have children learn more naturally, following their interests and working together in small groups.

We rented an old house and hired a head teacher. Many parents volunteered their services. I was one. I had been working part time at the Plainfield Science Center which was an outreach to underprivileged urban children. I had a real scientist as a supervisor. We had a lot of fun, hatching chickens, making soap and taking trips to the shore. I took that experience to Rainbow School and taught Science there.

Holly had a potter's wheel in the basement of our house. Mikki loved writing a diary and branched out to work on the school magazine. Gigi eventually joined up and learned to speak fluent French in another mother's back yard.

During this time, Zelik would take separate vacations. I would take the children on mine.

He refused to go to any kind of counseling done by a professional, but this was the self-help era, so we got into Couples Consciousness Raising.

It was strictly amateurs, but we tried to be honest with ourselves and each other. At least I did. I found out later that Zelik had bragged to the men that he had been seeing another woman, a petite blond that lived in Manhattan that he met on one of his solo vacations.

It was the summer I turned thirty three, 1969. We were well settled in the house in North Plainfield. We had belonged to a swim club since we moved there so that the children could have a place to swim and play over the summer. One of our friends invited a black activist from the Southern Christian Leadership Conference, as a guest, to the pool. At last they were integrating our swim club, sort of.

I had been watching the courageous nonviolent Civil Rights protest bus trips and marches. I had been appalled at the over- the-top violent response that the Southern whites, including their police, were greeting them with. I was stuck in the playroom on the ground floor of the house, watching TV and young children. Gigi would have been nine, Holly 8 and Mickey 6.

I was delighted that the movement had finally reached into my suburban bubble. I went over and introduced myself to James and told him of my support for the cause. He seems to have been more interested in how I looked in my bathing suit.

I had been living in survival mode, as I had when I came home from the hospital as a teen. I didn't trust Zelik anymore and my expectations of him had been drastically lowered. He didn't seem to want sex from me and I was just not getting any.

I was working for Weight Watchers as a lecturer and looked great. Of course that bathing suit had a lot of padding in the bust, which I figured helped balance my hips.

I was interested in Civil Rights. He was interested in me. He got my number from my friends and started to wage a concerted campaign to get me in bed. I held out as long as I could, but I was horny as hell and he eventually won.

He was only the second man I had sex with. I had remained faithful to my husband, in spite of a couple of other offers, but how could I refuse this hero of the war on racism and injustice?

I figure I was also a winner. James knew his way around a woman's body and I had never really experienced the "joy of sex" before.

Somehow, in my mind, the contract between Zelik and I had already been breached. I didn't feel particularly guilty going with James. We didn't even need to "sneak around". Zelik was not really interested in where I was or with whom. As long as he got what he wanted, he didn't seem to care. What he appeared to want was someone to take care of the children and the house and cook meals. He was not the least bit interested in contributing to that effort except with money.

Zelik was fine with me visiting my sister in Paris in 1966, when she was a student there. His mother was babysitting the children and taking care of him. I look back and think; I was just getting out of his way so he could do whatever he was doing, probably "catting around".

I was still seeing the Psychologist that I had been seeing since we had moved there. When I told him happily that I had taken a lover, he became upset and said I was "playing with fire". I knew that if I had been a man, he would be falling all over himself congratulating me. I realized that he had always been working for Zelik, since Zelik had paid the bills. He was also a "male chauvinist", just like most men.

James and I enjoyed each other for a while and then I began to think. He seemed to be falling in love with me; I could see no good coming of that. I needed to think of my children. I was pretty sure James had a wife out there somewhere or he would have asked me to marry him. I liked him and admired his courage but I wasn't in love with him. Even if I were, it was just not feasible to do anything about it.

I also did still care about Zelik. He was my first baby after all. I decided that I had to break it off with James, quickly and completely.

When I told him, James tried to talk me out of it. He said a black woman would have just leaned back and enjoyed the current situation. He was probably right, but I was determined.

I told Zelik about James. He didn't seem to want to know. It really shook him up. He planned to go to talk to my therapist the next time I went. I told James that and he decided he wanted to go there too.

James got there as I was sitting in the waiting room and Zelik was in the Psychologist's office. When Zelik came out and saw James there, he just fled. James didn't get to say a word, but if his aim was to size Zelik up, he had enough information to do that.

It was not easy to get James to let me go. He persisted in calling until I wouldn't answer his calls. If I heard his voice, I hung up. I saw his car circling my block. I just ignored it.

Finally, I was getting on a bus and he got on behind me and tried to talk to me. I had to "cut him dead". I looked through him. When the bus driver asked if he was bothering me, I said "No, just someone I used to know". James backed down the bus steps and left me alone after that.

I realize now that the affair was my first step out of that house. It seemed to tip the balance a bit between me and Zelik. Zelik had some symptoms after that and ended up "exhausted" at Carrier Clinic. Of course, he could not possibly admit they might be emotional symptoms.

Zelik recovered and we resumed the life we had, not quite together.

I had been taking courses to get my teaching certification. There was a teacher shortage and there were fast track programs.

Then I looked into the Goddard College External Degree Program. I could get a Masters degree while meeting with advisors and other students in the local area. All the time I needed to spend at Goddard, in Vermont, was one week each summer. I could take as long as I needed to complete the degree. It was perfect.

I started with wobbly knees. It had been a long time since I had been in school. I finished in two years. I ended up doing such a good job that my Core Advisor carried a copy of my very heavy Master's Thesis around for years after to show others how it was done. It was 1975.

The first family circa 1909
L to R: Louis, Regina, Jeanette, Jacob

Me running, Lorna in front, My dad, My mom , My Uncle Alvin in uniform and My Aunt Adeline. Circa 1943.

My Nana and me at the house in Leonia, reflecting, June, 1958

Regina in her little nest with Raggmopp Levin
Circa 1957

My family in the house in Glen Rock, December 1963: L-R Mom with Miriam, Dad with Holly, Zelik with Gigi. I was behind the camera.

Edna Sophie with kittens. Circa 1966

L to R Holly, Joy, Gigi, Mickey Circa 1969

Mom and Dad's 50th, 1982

Mikki and Holly in Tucson, Circa 1986

Ralph and I cut the cake at our Singles Club "reception"

"Beaming on the bema " Newlyweds September 4, 1992.

Melody, Gigi, Jeanette, Ralph outside Mom's house, Circa 1993

My Super family-with all the grandchildren. Circa 2004
L-R: Maryann and Paulo, Ralph, Holly. On couch: Dan, me, Gigi and Robby

Chapter Twelve

Piled Higher and Deeper

I declared my independence in 1976, the bicentennial of the Declaration of Independence of the now United States of America.

I had hung around well past the marriage's death date. I had made repeated efforts to resuscitate it to no avail. I was definitely not happy, and "when Momma ain't happy ain't nobody happy".

Zelik had finally told me to get lost. What he actually said was, "Do me a favor, go out and get laid."

I dropped him off, drove away and stopped at a roadside phone booth. I called my parent's house in Oradell. I told my mom I couldn't stay at the house in

North Plainfield, and asked if I could stay there that night.

My parents had never really liked Zelik. He had not made any effort to be nice or even polite to them. He would go off in another room and read or watch television when they came to visit. They tolerated him as long as I was determined to stay with him, but they were very happy to help in the getaway.

I made sure that the children knew where to reach me and that I was safe. They were all pretty independent by now and all enrolled in Rainbow School. Gigi was fifteen, Holly was thirteen and a half and Mikki was twelve and a half.

I cried the rest of the day and slept in my parent's spare bedroom that night. I was really expecting Zelik to call the next morning, but not a sound. I began to get used to the fact that it was over and even that it was a good thing that it was finally over.

Not only were the girls older, with the support system of the Rainbow School family, but I was, at last, both employed and fully credentialed.

I had just finished my Masters degree in Child Development, while working at the Summit Child Care Center as the Infant Care program teacher-director. I had started the program, which was in space in a church. I had used it as the basis of a "natural experiment" designed with the help of Edna Shapiro, PhD, a researcher at the Banks Street College of Education, my Goddard Field Faculty. I had found her in a footnote and was delighted that she agreed to work with me. If anyone wants to read my thesis, it is probably still in the College Library in Vermont.

I left Zelik during the summer break and was not actually working, although I was still getting paid. In August, I was notified that they were planning to move the Infant Care program to a new building and had decided to hire someone else to head it.

I was not particularly worried; since I knew I could get another job pretty easily, and I did.

In the meantime, I set up a new home for myself and my daughters. I rented an apartment in a relatively safe residential neighborhood in nearby Plainfield, on the second floor of a private home. It had room for all of the children, but they had ideas of their own. They thought someone should stay with their dad. Gigi was the designee. Holly was angry at me, but agreed to live with me for the sake of Mikki.

Gigi had to make up some work in order to get into North Plainfield High School. I had gotten her into the Summer School program at Rutgers Prep, a very fine private school. She loved the place and they loved her.

Later Gigi told me she didn't like North Plainfield High School. Due to overcrowding, the High School was on split sessions. Gigi told me that she was getting out so early that there was no one home and nothing for her to do. She had been getting into a social scene she didn't like as a consequence. The kids were taking drugs and having sex in the middle of the day and they were pressuring her to do the same.

Rutgers Prep was happy to take Gigi and gave her a half tuition scholarship. She was picked up by the school's bus in nearby Plainfield and taken to the campus in Somerset New Jersey . In the afternoon she was dropped off at the bus stop.

This worked out quite well as long as Zelik was living in the house in North Plainfield.

Before my side of the bed had gotten cold, he had moved in his petite blond girlfriend. Now I knew. Unfortunately, so did the kids who were still in the house. He might not have been having sex with me, but he had it loudly with her, with my kids as an audience.

She didn't last long. She hadn't known Zelik was married. She met him on one of his separate vacations in the Catskills. I had the kids and he had her. It had gone on quite a while after that. When I took his Volvo, because it was the smaller of the two cars, I found a pile of unpaid traffic tickets from her neighborhood in Manhattan. I also found an ant colony. He was a slob.

Then the house was sold according to the divorce agreement and the money split. Zelik's share of the notes from the sale of Margie's Cake Box was also split. I didn't want alimony, I was a Feminist. I asked for child support and got it, although Zelik didn't pay very reliably. He didn't want to give me a dime.

We had come to a compromise, with the help of his cousin the lawyer. The notes were split five ways. Each of the children got a share, but that money was only to be used for their education. One share was for Zelik and one for me, but they were to be the last distributed.

When the money from the sale of the house came through, it was the occasion for a sigh of relief for me. We had already moved to Teaneck, N.J.

Holly had aged out of Rainbow School and was in the very well-recommended Teaneck Alternative High School. Mikki was in Thomas Jefferson Junior High.

Gigi was still in Rutgers Prep, but by then her father had married a black midwife named Nicole and moved to public housing in Plainfield. (He was ripping off the taxpayers. I know he had more money than would have been allowed. He had always been in cash businesses where you could pretend not to have money and hide it behind the fridge. That was why my lawyer went for the notes.)

Unfortunately, that meant that Gigi had to walk through a not so nice neighborhood in Plainfield to get to and from the Rutgers Prep bus.

When we first moved to Teaneck we lived in a lovely old apartment building. It had only five apartments. Ours had a fireplace in the dining area and in the living room, nice high ceilings, lots of light and lots of space. I let Mikki move her upright piano into her bedroom and paint it purple.

One night I got a call from Gigi, please come and pick her up. She could no longer live with her father.

We jerry-rigged a way for her to get to Rutgers Prep, but it was such a difficult commute and she had been through so much, she didn't last quite through her Senior year. Eventually, they gave her credit and she was listed as a graduate.

We had planned a trip to California by bus when the money from the housc came through. Gigi really wanted to go, but she ended up in Bergen Pines County Hospital.

When she was first admitted, I went over there to be with her. I was holding her, when who should walk in but the Psychologist from North Plainfield. He offered condolences on the end of my marriage and warned me that it was "inappropriate" to be holding her. He implied sexual connotations.

Well, I really let him have it. I told him that I was her mother and when my daughter is in pain there is nothing inappropriate about me holding her. I also told him that he should be congratulating me for being out of that awful marriage and expressed clearly what I thought of his male chauvinist thinking.

That felt good. Of course, having yelled at him, he probably still thought I was crazy.

Chapter Thirteen

Sex and The Single Mom

When I had my two girls all set in the apartment on the second floor of the two-family house in Plainfield and Gigi had started High School in North Plainfield, I had a few moments to breathe.

It was 1976 and I was turning 40. I was going to do a double birthday celebration with another mother from Rainbow School but that fell through. I still felt as though I had a lot to celebrate.

When I first went to a lawyer, I wasn't sure I wanted a divorce. I started out talking about a legal separation. The lawyer looked at me and said, "When it is over it is over." He was so right.

He pointed out that Zelik was in a cash business and it would be easy for him to hide income. He asked about other possible assets. There was the house and of course, the notes. That was the notes from the sale of Margie's Cake Box. My lawyer cheered up considerably and declared that he would "blow his doors off!" I knew I had found the right lawyer.

When Zelik got the papers and realized I was serious, he looked for a lawyer, not in the phone book but in the family. Sure enough, one of his cousins was a lawyer, having newly graduated law school. He was not a specialist in matrimonial law, but he was his cousin and could be expected to be loyal to Zelik.

He saw pretty quickly that Zelik was being unreasonable. He didn't want me to have a penny, not even to buy groceries for his daughters. He tried to talk sense to Zelik and explained to him that no judge was going to take the same punishing attitude towards me that he was.

My lawyer encouraged me to negotiate with Zelik. I met with him in places like diners to put a damper on his anger and mine and possibly keep him from stalking out. That didn't really help. It took his cousin telling him that the compromise was fair and did not advantage me.

The compromise was that I would get some child support, not a lot because I was working. I didn't ask for alimony. It was against my principles, plus it was not tax deductable.

What made it all possible were the notes. Zelik had half of the notes from the sale of the bakery coming to him. The other half went to his former partner, Bill. They were to be paid off over time. His cousin suggested that Zelik's share be split five ways. Each of the children would get a share and Zelik and I would each get a share after the others had been distributed.

Zelik still didn't like that I was going to get anything at all. His cousin explained that it didn't work that way. Zelik liked my suggestion that we put in the provision that the children's notes could only be used for their education. I figured I could feed them with my income and the child support. He agreed and we had an uncontested divorce.

There were times when I had difficulty feeding and maintaining the three of them. Zelik was not very good about paying the child support. I remember asking my sister for a loan. She was single and working and at that point I was unemployed again.

Lorna gave me a $20 bill, told me to put it in my car for emergencies and not to ask her for more. I was humiliated and angry. She obviously had no idea what real life was about.

My parents came through for me. They gave me a loan with no limit and due for payment when I got on my feet, whenever that was or never, if necessary. I called them the Bank of Mom and Dad and paid back every penny eventually.

The children all did use the note money to further their education. I counted room and board as part of the expenses of an education, but they had to be in school.

Once I could breathe, I started dating again. The last time I had "dated" was in the 1950s. I didn't count James, because he had found me.

Now I had to find suitable men and it wasn't easy. There were some ads in newspapers, there were singles newsletters with other ads but mostly you had to go to groups that met in churches and such. There was Parents Without Partners which seemed to attract men much older than me. Younger men apparently considered themselves to be eligible bachelors and didn't relate to being parents. Why should they? The vast majority of their children were with their mothers. I did meet one dad who was trying to get custody, but it was very hard in those days.

I met a seemingly very suitable man, an engineer. He was intelligent and well spoken. He even agreed to meet with some of my Rainbow School friends. They were impressed.

Unfortunately, when I did go to bed with him, which in the seventies seemed to be expected in a much shorter time frame than it was in the fifties, I found out that he was not really single. He and his wife had an "open marriage". They had no children and had agreed to "see" other people. He seemed to think it was great for the marriage.

I didn't have to worry about contraception. Years before I had a hysterectomy due to a huge fibroid. I did not have to worry about venereal diseases because we thought they were all curable. Sex in the seventies seemed simple but finding love was not.

While I was still in Plainfield I met Gene. He was tall and seemed to wear his small car. He had a boat down at the shore and a Camper truck to get back and forth. He was nine years younger than me but didn't look it. He too was an engineer. We hit it off right away. He took me out for dinner. We were supposed to go to a fancy place. He didn't want to be valet-parked and parked himself. Then we walked in to the restaurant and the vibes were all wrong. They seemed to think they were doing us a favor in allowing us to be seated. We looked at each other. I said maybe we should try another place. He seemed to think I had read his mind. We went to a quaint hotdog joint that he loved and had a great time.

When I moved to Teaneck, he did not find it too far to go to see me. He would pick me up in his Camper and take me to his boat. He eventually bought a bigger boat on which we could sleep. We were in love.

Even though he had met my daughters and knew that they were having lots of problems at that time, that didn't stop him from wanting to be with me. I wanted to be with him too, and even considered marrying him.

He never asked me. I understood why. His father was dead. He was the only child and his mother was not well. She had taken care of him when he was a tiny premature child and made sure he survived. He had to take care of her now. He never introduced me to her.

I also loved him enough to consider that if he married me he would never have children. He was still young. Someday he would find a woman younger than me that could give him children. I am pretty sure he did.

I had to let him go. It was tough because we were so attracted to each other, but I did.

After Gene, I didn't have much luck, but for quite a while my children's problems consumed my energy and I didn't have as much time to "date".

Chapter Fourteen

Sophie's Story

If I would have had a granddaughter, her name would have been Sophie after my mother-in-law, Edna Sophie Slabinski Shulman. She was my children's grandmother and my friend. One of my mother's sayings was, "To have a friend is to be one." I was her friend too. I learned to love her over the years.

Edna's story is a tragic one. I would like to learn more about her family of origin. Her father told my children that they left Russia because of the pogroms. He was a tailor.

All I know so far is that Edna was known as Sophie, her middle name and a more ethnically correct one for her early life. She was a talented pianist at an early age. I find it intriguing that in an immigrant family money was found to give her piano lessons.

Sophie had sex with her second cousin Solik when she was seventeen and conceived a son, who I will call Zelik. He was my first and now ex-husband.

I have little good to say about him and since he is still alive, I am taking precautions against a libel suit

Sophie was pregnant in 1935, there was no legal, safe abortion available and she was forever "damaged goods".

Cousin Solik would have to marry her, and he did. His idea of marriage was based on a common interpretation which involved him getting lots of services from her and him supporting her and the child. He was not strictly obligated to be faithful to her as “boys will be boys”. Of course since they both came from Orthodox Jewish families, they were still technically subject to the anti-adultery clause.

I remember Sophie’s father. He came to live with us briefly as a very old man. He was quiet and sweet. I remember Solik’s father too. He was the template for his son and grandson.

Sophie and Solik's model of marriage was the Masochist and the Sadist. Sophie was warm and loving in an overboard kind of way.

When my children were young, she lived nearby and dropped by often. She seemed to feel she needed to buy their love by bringing gifts every time she came. I eventually had to sit down with her and tell her that it was not only unnecessary; it was bad for the children. She reluctantly agreed to only bring gifts for birthdays and Hanukkah/Christmas.

Solik was an abuser. I think he limited himself to verbal and emotional abuse but he was terribly good at it. He was also a womanizer.

He was always nice to me. Being a young attractive woman probably didn't hurt. He doted on his grandchildren and the fact that they were all girls probably didn't hurt either.

I was an eye witness to Solik's cruelty to Sophie (who by this time wanted to be called Edna). I remember vividly one incident when she had bought a set of nice luggage for herself. Solik went ballistic when he found out. He was making very good money, so that was not the problem. Apparently, she had gotten "uppity" and had to be beaten down.

She kept making excuses for him and imagining he was “mellowing”. In the meantime he was “chasing tail”. She finally found him in bed with another woman.

I loved her and,as a fellow Shulman wife, felt an increasing kinship to her; as Zelik reverted to his father’s pattern with me.

Edna confided to me that Solik had made her have an abortion when Zelik was only about a year and a half old. She regretted that as a consequence, she could no longer bear children.

She had no idea how many alarm bells that revelation set off in me. I was an early childhood person. I pictured Solik yelling that she had to “get rid of the baby” with super bright, super sensitive baby Zelik within earshot.

Edna had also previously told me that she had resented the baby and it took her about a year and a half to take pity on him and show him some affection. Of course it was obvious that she then overcompensated, a natural reaction, with plenty of guilt for fuel and the knowledge that he would be her only child.

When I first met her, Sophie was very much beaten down. I am now reminded of my friend Kathy's marriage. I had seen the cultural influences and norms that made that exploitive of Kathy, but there was little resemblance. That was a middle class marriage. Solik was not middle class; he was, to be kind, working class, and coarse, not the least bit "refined".

Solik worked with his hands as a baker and made a good living. He supported his wife and son, but he had few other interests that I could discern. He did love to dance and went out to ballroom dancing venues, without his wife, and picked up women. His cruising name was "Charlie".

I had lost all the excess weight and was looking great. I had some nice clothes because I was lecturing for Weight Watchers. I forget what the occasion was that I bought the dress for, but I will always remember the scoop necked, form fitting red satin dress.

Solik asked me to go dancing with him and wear the dress. He said he wanted to tease his ballroom buddies and make them think he had been able to pick up a beautiful young woman, young enough to be his daughter.

I loved dancing and was very good at it. Zelik wasn't and couldn't have cared less about dancing. He didn't mind a bit if I went out with "Charlie", as long as he didn't have to babysit.

I had a great time and so did Solik. It was one time only but to be remembered for a lifetime.

Solik liked me and was always nice to me. When I first left his son, I was surprised when he offered to let me stay with my youngest, Mikki, in his then vacant apartment in Elizabeth. He had moved in with his then girlfriend and didn't need it.

My other two daughters chose to stay in the house with their father and his girlfriend, for the time being.

I saw Sophie change over the years. She was now called Edna. After she found Solik in bed with another woman, she finally faced that he was not "mellowing" and was not going to.

She went back to school and obtained a degree and certification in Special Education. She worked as a teacher of extremely challenged children and seemed to have found her niche.

She eventually got a divorce and lived on her own. She was still devoted to her granddaughters and would take them places in her car. I know she regretted it, but after we divorced, she was loyal to her son and avoided seeing me.

We were already living in the two-family house in Teaneck. I think Gigi was up at Goddard College. One day when Holly and Mikki came home, I gathered them in Holly's room and had to tell them that their beloved Grandma had been killed.

She was shot in a holdup of Nikki's, the little store that Zelik had set his new wife Nichole up in. Edna had been minding the store for them. She was shot in the head and killed instantly.

At her funeral, I was sitting in the middle of the auditorium where the service was held, with Gigi. Holly and Mikki sat in the first row with their father, Nicole and her family. She had a few children. I never got to know them.

When the service was over, Edna's sister Mary confronted Solik and lost any composure she had managed to maintain. She yelled at him for treating her sister so abominably and spit in his face. Yes!

I think her grandmother's death was especially traumatic for Holly. She went off on me on an answering machine tape, after she had left the house at 18. She accused me of dishonoring her grandmother's memory. Of all the things she said on that tape, none of them complimentary, that is the thing that hurt the most.

Solik lived long enough to meet and marry the woman of his dreams. She did not live long, however. She died in his arms on a dance floor in Florida.

Chapter Fifteen

Dominoes

Gigi broke down when we were still in the apartment building. She was in Bergen Pines when we went to California by bus. What fun Holly and Mikki had on the trip and in California! It was the first time I could afford a vacation in some time. The money had come through from the sale of the house.

I managed to have fun too, knowing that Gigi was in good hands and had no chance of getting out in the short time we would be away. I promised her a trip with me when she was better and I delivered. We eventually went to Puerto Rico together.

My younger two had been in the Teaneck schools for almost a year when my lease on the apartment came due. They told me that they couldn't bring their new friends to an apartment, even a cool one with two fireplaces. All their friends lived in private homes, one fancier than the other.

I looked for and quickly found an apartment on the ground floor of a two-family house on Queen Anne Rd. The owner, also a divorced woman, lived alone upstairs. We didn't have dogs and the children were old enough to appear not to be too much trouble, so she signed us up.

Little did any of us know how much trouble middle class adolescent girls could be!

After losing the job at Summit Infant Care, I got a job at the YM/WHA in Union, NJ. It was fairly close to Plainfield, but I had a long commute from Teaneck down the NJ Turnpike.

I got the opportunity to head up the Nursery School. There was a Day Care Center at the Y also, with a different director. That was on a federal contract and only took children from low income families.

I introduced day care for the Nursery School population, as more and more middle class and even affluent families began to need their women to work.

Then, I introduced Infant Day Care. After dealing with the affluent parents in Summit, I was sure the program would do well in Union. They took a chance on me and it was not only a pioneering effort for the Y, it was a huge success.

Ten years later I was invited to a brunch in my honor at the Y. I was treated to bagels and kind words as well as a look at the babies I had first brought in as sizable children. I proudly brought my parents, who were completely dazzled and delighted.

Everyone deserves a little recognition. I have remembered that in my later life and have been involved in giving awards to many women who would have been serving in silence otherwise.

One day I got a call while at a Y staff meeting. My daughter Mikki was in a South Bronx police precinct house. Would I come and pick her up?

I raced over there and found the place. The South Bronx looked like a bombed-out part of a foreign city. Those were the days of high crime and urban blight.

The story was that Mikki was offered a ride to get some pot and she accepted it, only to find herself stuck on the street with no ride home. She must have looked out of place because the police soon found her and took her to the station. The cop in charge actually said to me, "What is a nice girl like her doing in a place like this?" Yes, ritzy Teaneck had drugs and all the other problems that young people faced elsewhere.

Holly had a strange relationship with a young man who later stalked and killed his ex girlfriend, right behind one of the prosperous stores on Cedar Lane, Teaneck's main street.

Mikki was the first to use some of the education money from the notes. She wanted to take a modeling course and said that she could work as a model to help her get through college.

Mikki was strikingly good looking in her early teens and had made quite a splash on the Teaneck social scene.

She had almost immediately gotten accepted in the "popular kids" crowd and had a prestigious jock boyfriend. I had my doubts about modeling school, but I couldn't counter Mikki's logic.

Mikki, thank goodness, just wasn't that person. She eventually saw through the shallow value system of the whole modeling thing. She also saw through the shallow "popular kids" culture.

In the meantime, Holly was very angry at me. When we first moved to the house on Queen Anne Rd, she was very loving and cooperative. Then something seemed to shift in her thinking and I was the master villain in the melodrama. Everything that had gone wrong, including her grandmother's death seemed to be my fault.

I admit that I had lost any illusions about my ex when he failed to protect Gigi to the point that she came home to me in pieces.

I have always been outspoken and I couldn't shut up completely about the late child support and her father's other obvious failings. As to my mother-in-law's death, she gave her life minding his store in Plainfield that no one in their right mind would have rented. It was a high crime area!

In any case, Holly claims to this day that the divorce did not traumatize her, I did.

My theory is that the divorce was like an earthquake followed by a tsunami. The original "train wreck" theory got upgraded when that actually happened somewhere in Southeast Asia.

All three of my children were affected by the breakup of the marriage. Gigi was directly affected because she stayed in the North Plainfield house with her father and his blond girl friend and eventually in the subsidized apartment with her father and his new wife. She had no problem with my opinion of her father. She had been directly injured by him. She slid over to my side of the fence.

Holly wanted desperately to hold on to her father in spite of his rapidly developing track record. She knew that she could yell at me as much as she wanted and she would never lose me. She was not so sure about her father.

He had remarried rather rapidly. His new wife already had a clutch of children. He then got her pregnant. They found out with Amniocentesis that the child had Down's Syndrome. I don't know what Nicole had to say about it, but Zelik said he wanted to bring the pregnancy to term anyway, and she did.

Mikki now says that she felt replaced by her Father's new family. My theory is that at the time, she stayed on the fence and Holly slid over to her father's side.

Gigi hardly lived in Teaneck at all. She got out of Bergen Pines and soon went up to Goddard College in Vermont. I had seen the campus and sampled the philosophy. I felt it was the perfect place for Gigi to continue her education and her recovery. It was too expensive for her note to cover four years there. After two wonderful years she came back home and went to Montclair State until she graduated.

Holly broke down briefly a couple of times, the major feature of which was anger at me. She stayed only a few days each time at Holy Name Hospital in Teaneck.

That was the second domino and I became sure that Mikki would be next. I took her to counseling with Catholic Charities. That was all I could afford. I never made much money.

The nun, (who did not wear a habit), saw Mikki, heard my story and kept saying there was nothing wrong with her and nothing she could do.

Of course, I was right. It didn't happen right away, but when the younger two were out of high school, Gigi was in college and Holly had moved out.

We had moved to Weehawken. I was working in Manhattan by then and it made my commute to my new job easier. Then, Mikki fell apart. She ended up in St. Mary's Hospital in Hoboken. She was the last domino.

When she got out, I set her up in a rooming house and arranged for her to go to Ramapo College in Rockland County, NY. Remember, I couldn't use the note money unless she was in school. Later, Holly, who had gotten set up in Tucson, Arizona, invited Mikki to join her.

Holly had moved out as soon as she was 18 leaving a mess in the basement of the house in Teaneck. Gigi and I had to clean it up. We were moving and couldn't leave it the way it was.

At first, Holly lived with her boyfriend who supported them with three jobs as a car parker. She then found work and eventually realized that it would take her a very long time to make any kind of a decent living.

Yielding to my "unreasonable" rule that she had to be in school to get any kind of financial support from me, she enrolled in nearby Fairleigh Dickenson University.

Soon she found out she was a talented student (no surprise). She transferred to Alfred State College in upstate New York for their Ceramic Engineering major. She is now a Ceramic Engineer and a PhD Chemical Engineer; "my daughter the doctor".

Holly has made her peace with me, but we have had to agree to disagree about our conflicting theories on the effects of the divorce.

Chapter Sixteen

"Such Devoted Sisters"

My sister, who I will call Lorna, had enthusiastically embraced the idea of her only daughter Melody being bat mitzvah. She made sure she got to the classes and the Temple services. Not an easy task, because Melody was kept so busy. I used to say she didn't have a life, she had a schedule.

Lorna also kept in touch with and cultivated the extended family, and subsequently got a good attendance at the bat mitzvah. Melody did a beautiful job during the service, reading the torah and giving a thoughtful presentation.

Lorna and Melody's father Stewart were divorced and Lorna made a point of letting everyone know that she was paying for the entire proceedings. He attended the service, looking handsome on the bema, but he was not at the reception.

The first thing I remember about the reception was Lorna walking around with a big platter of jumbo shrimp. Even a lot of gentiles know that shrimp is not kosher, but this was a very Reform reception. What I found inappropriate was that she was serving the shrimp herself and bragging with each one she "sold" how expensive they were.

My new husband, Ralph, and I were seated with my Uncle Alvin and his second wife Louise. He was already ill with lung cancer and it was the last time I saw him alive. My Uncle Herman was there but his beloved Connie was ill and it was a sacrifice. My dad was already gone and my mother's mind was going. It was the end of an era. But "the show must go on".

My sister was all pervasive. Aside from assisting the wait staff with the shrimp, she interviewed all the kids for a video tape and emceed a cake lighting extravaganza. We had not been getting along and I did not want to participate. I was forced to go up and light a candle to the tune of “We are such devoted sisters”.

The topper was when Linda, usurping a custom usually reserved for weddings, forced a small group of male guests to lift her up and carry her around in a chair. Now, she was no lightweight. I was afraid my Cousin Jerry, who was in his late fifties, was going to have a heart attack. Luckily, he did not have to have an ambulance upstage my sister on her precarious perch; but ever since, Ralph and I have called it the "Big Butt Mitzvah".

My dad died in Florida in 1991 on February 8th, his eighty-second birthday.

My sister and I had been down there a little before his death and knew it was coming. There had been no severe long term illness. I think he was weakened by a cold and it went into Pneumonia. Then all his systems began to fail. He had also just had the stress of having to relocate from the original apartment they had sublet to another. I forget what was wrong with the first one.

My parents had been “snow birds” for many years. They used to take a two-bedroom apartment in a retirement development for about four months a year. Whether I wanted to or not, some years they insisted I go and visit them down there and soak up the beneficial sun. I don't really like Florida; it is too hot and flat. I don't like retirement developments either, even now that I am retired; too many old people, no children.

My mother was in shock and allowed my sister to arrange the funeral. Lorna emceed the proceedings and gave a maudlin speech. She had placed pictures of my father around the room, something Jews just don't do. (It's that graven image thing.) She had also raided my father's desk and found some old memorabilia including potty joke telegrams business acquaintances had sent him on the occasion of my birth. She had that stuff out too. She also placed a bottle of his favorite scotch and some good cigars in the coffin. Also inappropriate, but of that I approved.

My father was definitely Jewish and his religion meant a lot to him. It is because of him that I am still Jewish. I cherish an old edition of the Union Prayer Book, (the Reform Jewish version) with our old Forest Hills address in the front. On the inside cover, in dad's handwriting , it says "12/10/43 To my darling daughters Gertrude Joy and Lorna Carol May this bring to them the same fond memories that I hold dear when my father would say his 'kiddish' on the many cherished Friday evenings Dad".

I read from that prayer book in the hospital when my mother was dying. She had outlived all her siblings and her friends. She was 91 and deep into Alzheimer's but I think she appreciated it.

My mother left detailed instructions for her "arrangements" she didn't want a fancy funeral. She had admired the simplicity and dignity of Adeline's "graveside only" service and adopted the format. Unlike the elaborate coffin Adeline had, Jeanette asked for a plain pine box. It had a Jewish star on it.

Jews don't do flowers, but I couldn't help myself. Her middle name was Rose, so it was a giant bouquet of white roses.

Lorna was nowhere to be found when my mother died. She was on one of her many trips or vacations. She hadn't left me a number. I even tried calling Stewart's daughter in England to find her.

The Rabbi and the woman Cantor, from the temple that Lorna belonged to, came to the gravesite. For a pregnant Gigi, Ralph and me, they intoned the beautiful ancient words.

In the same night table drawer as the prayer book, I have been keeping a note from my sister dated 1-9-91 (almost exactly a month before dad died).

Lorna had gotten me in for half of the cost of a leaf on the “Tree of Life” in her temple, inscribed to our parents. It must still be there.

She did not wait for me to be around to tell them about it. Just as well, under the circumstances. In the note Lorna told me that my dad was very moved and said, “It’s just you feel everyone will forget you when you’re gone.”

No, we haven’t forgotten. As he used to sing, “A good man is hard to find, you always get the other kind”. He was a good man, a proud boy scout, the model for Horton the Elephant, faithful 100%.

Chapter Seventeen

Helping My Mother Down The Hill

When I complained about how hard it was to walk up the steep hill from the ferry in St. George, a friend pointed out that it is harder to walk down.

The signs were there earlier, but they became more and more apparent. Holly was married during the summer of 1991; (just before I met Ralph).It was outdoors, in upstate New York near Alfred, at a friend's place called "Pollywog Holler". Jeanette was seated next to my ex father-in-law. He said she kept asking him the same questions over and over.

Jeanette had tried going back to Florida on her own soon after my father died but it just hadn't worked. So in the winter of 1992 Ralph and I took her to Arizona, where with a lot of help from Mikki, who was living in Tucson, we tried to find an assisted living place where she would be comfortable for at least part of the winter.

We took a suite at a nice motel. During the night my mother wandered out and, according to the desk clerk, tried to take a bus. We found a letter from a doctor in her purse indicating that she had Alzheimer's. We couldn't figure out why Lorna hadn't told us. She had taken her to the doctor. Not surprisingly, the Arizona experiment didn't succeed and we had to put my mother on a plane to be picked up by Lorna in Newark.

Lorna had noticed that my mother was not paying her bills and went in and took over her finances. She signed her up for an Adult Day Care program.

One day we got a call from Jeanette that she had fallen and hurt herself. She said she was alone and couldn't reach Lorna who lived 20 minutes away. We hurried over from Staten Island, about an hour away, to find mom had some minor abrasions, no broken bones, and had not broken the skin. She had slipped on a too zealously waxed floor and panicked.

I became convinced that mom needed more supervision. She couldn't manage being alone and there was the danger of her wandering out at night. I thought that it was time for Lorna and me to assess the situation and work together to provide appropriate care. The first step would be to find out what assets our mother had so we could figure out how they could best be used to meet her needs.

Well, I apparently hit a nerve. Lorna made it clear that there was no team approach, no "we" or "our" in her scheme of things. She was in charge and I had no right to interfere. She refused to share any financial information.

Under pressure, Lorna devised an elaborate patchwork of Aides to cover the hours before and after the Adult Day Care, but Jeanette was left alone from 8PM to 9AM. This was getting complicated and expensive. I finally felt I had to go to court.

I didn't want it but it turned out a Competency Hearing was the only way to go. Then, hopefully, I could find out how much money my mother had and how long she could afford this lifestyle.

My mother couldn't remember anything and relied on a huge wall calendar that hung in the kitchen. I kept the last two pages because some of the entries were so bizaare. I didn't think anyone would believe what went on:

1995, JANUARY: At the top, "**DON'T SEE JOY OR TALK TO JOY** Hang up! Joy is suing you". On the bottom "**HANG UP ON JOY**" and in my mother's handwriting above it "My lawyer said".

In the space for January 27, "**COURT DATE (JOY IS SUING TO TAKE OVER YOUR $ & CARE) IT COST YOU $3000 SO FAR) LORNA TAKES YOU TO COURT**" I had crossed out the $3000 line and had written next to it "Liar, Liar, pants on fire!" That was for Lorna. The whole thing was too complex for my mother by this time anyway.

In court my mother did a beautiful acting job. She always agreed with the last thing she heard and had been carefully coached by Lorna. She said she felt Lorna, who lived closer, should have custodianship.

Well, the judge went along. Lorna won. One little catch, I was to be given the financial information I had been seeking. A court appointed attorney would have temporary charge of my mother's finances until that was accomplished.

It turned out Lorna couldn't manage to give it to him any more than she could to me. He finally made some sense of her jumbled reports and I got the information; but under the circumstances, Lorna backed down and let me have both Physical and Financial custody.

Written across the bottom of the August 1995 page of my mother's calendar: "**YOUR LICENSE IS REVOKED DO NOT DRIVE"**. The neighbors had complained that Jeanette was a menace to their children when she drove into the little cul-de-sac she lived on. Lorna finally wrote to the DMV and got her license revoked. Later, Ralph and I took her car to the dealer to sell. She had not been maintaining it and it was a menace too.

On the top of the September 1995 page: **"The Court ordered you must have someone sleep over every night. Pat sleeps over Monday through Friday. My friend Maria sleeps over Saturday and Sunday. Please don't give money to anyone. Be sweet to them please."**

"The BUS PICKS YOU UP MONDAY TO FRIDAY AT 9ish".

I kept the patch-work Aide schedule in place when I took over as my mother's guardian. It became harder and harder to get people, especially for the night shift.

My mother didn't want to bathe and it became increasingly difficult and dangerous to try to get her in the tub. It was not that she was frail and weak, on the contrary; she was pretty fit and, pumped full of adrenaline, she could deck you.

I had kept her in the little cottage on Garden Place as long as I could. She was getting increasingly difficult and her financial condition demanded that we sell her house, the only sizable asset she had left.

With the house sold and the money invested, she had enough to live as long as she could. Her ambition was to make it to 100.

We had looked at Assisted Living places in Bergen County when my mother was in better shape. They were swanky and extremely expensive. Now that I was guardian, I looked in Staten Island. I found a small place near the FDR memorial boardwalk that goes from the Verrazano Narrows Bridge in South Beach to Midland Beach; New Broadview Manor. It was "hamisha" or homey, owned by Russian immigrants.

The Manager was from (…drum roll please,) Romania. The customer relations person was a warm, genuine young woman who won all our hearts immediately, including Jeanette's. After our visit and tour I asked her if she would like to live here. She said "yes".

The patch-work plan failed just before we got my mom into New Broadview. She stayed with us for a few days, sleeping on our pull out couch.

She was taking medication to keep her from getting agitated. It didn't always work, but for this visit, she was a pussycat. (I didn't try to give her a bath.)

I think she was genuinely happy. We looked over old photos and she recognized just about all the people in them. I enjoyed the time with her too. It wasn't planned, but maybe that visit provided a smooth transition to New Broadview.

She had a private room, so she had two closets. She had her own furniture: her beautiful dresser and matching night table, the bright flowered chair from her living room and her small nesting tables. On the walls were many of the paintings she had done; most prominently the portraits of her and dad.

I got her a small TV on a swivel to sit on the night table. The connection to the antenna was bad, so it didn't work that well, but it didn't matter. She couldn't really use it or even the phone. Her connection with modern technology seems to have been severed; but she was never alone, she was well taken care of and before long, even had a "boyfriend". (It was a short lived affair, he died soon after.)

I was still working and was out in the field a lot, so I was able to visit relatively frequently. Ralph and I took her out for lunch every weekend.

Somewhat surprisingly, Lorna visited only a few times in the over three years mom was there. She did show up after mom died to take home most of what was in the room. The staff had to stop her from taking home the bed.

I gave some of the paintings to Aides. I kept the self-portrait of my mom. Lorna claimed the one of my dad.

Chapter Eighteen

Spider Woman

Margaret Mead, one of my heroes, said that you should find work at what you would do anyway even if you didn't get paid. I was able to do that, even if my mother was right and I got "paid in the dark".

Things have changed only a little in the Early Childhood Education field in the US. I am pretty sure that the Director of the Early Childhood Department of the YMCA that I go to now is the only one with a Certification in Early Childhood Education and the only one who makes an even half-way decent salary. The Y doesn't have day care. It is way too expensive to run properly, especially infant day care.

The City of New York, under its new very liberal Mayor Di Blasio, has introduced "Universal Pre K".That is a wonderful step ahead, but it isn't universal day care.

What I said in my Master's Thesis in 1975 is still true. The rest of the developed world is way ahead of us, not only in Healthcare but also in providing safe, educational and nurturing care for their youngest citizens while enabling their women to contribute fully to the economy.

Women have some choices to make that men don't Many are still forced to either endure extreme poverty or get a partner to help them raise their offspring.

Unfortunately, getting a partner doesn't always help much economically and sometimes makes things worse. The choice of whether to bear offspring, under the circumstances that prevail at the time that they are harboring a fetus, should be the woman's alone. Only she can know whether there is any kind of a chance for that potential child to get what it needs, should it be brought to term.

Women are still being encouraged to be romantics, like I was when I was in my late teens and early 20s. Many of them are just not buying it any more. There has been progress, but many simply don't see it as such.

My head was filled with romantic ballads like "Blue Moon" and "My Funny Valentine", and movies in which everyone had to be paired off, making it a happy ending.

Young women are not finding it a problem to be "standing alone" at the threshold of life. They have lots of dreams in their hearts and don't have to wait for some man to give one to them.

Only a man can be funny looking and expect to get praised for it. Women still work very hard to conform to impossible air-brushed images.

I don't consider rap to be music. It does seem to glorify crime and put women down, but it can't be worse in its effects on women than the stuff we had our heads full of in the fifties.

Rap is full of all the common terms of abuse of women: bitch, (a female dog), son of a bitch, bastard, (the out of wedlock child of a bitch) etc. Can't a man be really despicable without his mother being implicated? How can we wonder at the high rate of actual physical abuse of women?

When I was first divorced I needed a job and went to get certified as a substitute teacher in all the local school systems. In Plainfield, I was surprised and upset that they expected me to sign a loyalty oath. This was something left over from McCarthy and the fifties. I had not suspected that it could still be around in the seventies. I needed work, but I was not willing to submit to that outdated injustice. I left my outstanding resume and application and respectfully refused to sign the oath. They decided to waive it. I was hired anyway.

I went to work as a permanent sub for a fifth grade teacher who had been driven to a nervous breakdown by the very class I was taking over.

The Plainfield Public Schools reflected the urban nature of that city. North Plainfield, where we had lived, was part of the suburban "white ring" around it that some thought was strangling it.

My class was overwhelmingly black. The boys were mostly older than would be expected because they had been "left back" a year or two. They were almost all taller than me.

I figure I was hired because I was not right out of school. The Principal was a tough black woman who immediately tried to toughen me up.

When I had first joined the job market, I had been treated to a course in "Assertiveness Training" by the government. Many older women were joining the workforce and had to overcome their acculturation to being submissive and "nice".

This was the graduate course and aimed at helping me control the classroom and keep order.

I was an open classroom teacher and I was not going to settle for just keeping order. I established myself and did what I could to build the self esteem of those very beaten-down young people. While I was doing that, I tried to find a way to teach them something too.

I found out that there was a beautiful park nearby and the weather was warm so I took the whole class out to the park outfitted to explore nature.

I found out that one young man, who could hardly read, excelled at catching frogs. All of them could collect specimens and water samples. We were off!

At the end of the term I wanted to give all of them some kind of award, some bit of recognition. I ordered enough award certificates for all of them. However, by the time we got to the award ceremony, unknown to me, the number of my awards had been cut in half. The boy who was to be recognized for catching frogs was stiffed and so were many others. I was devastated and so were they. I apologized to the class when we got back to our room. The "system" had failed us all.

Before we left Plainfield, I got a job as Nursery School Teacher-Director at the YM/WHA in Union. I was in charge of the program but it was a "part-time job" (30 hours a week) and offered no benefits.

These were mostly white but very urban kids. There was no nearby farm, so one of the first things I did was take them, with some parent helpers, on a field trip to a giant farmers' market. It was a big success.

While we were there, I sat down on a crate to rest a minute. At the time, I thought I had gotten a splinter, but I was bitten by a spider. It was not an ordinary spider; it was a deadly Brown Recluse, also known as a "fiddle back" spider because of the shape of its markings. They are very tiny and very shy but their bite can kill.

It took a while for me to realize that it was serious. By then we had moved to Teaneck and I was commuting to Union and back on the Turnpike.

I ended up stopping every other day at the office of the doctor I had seen when my parents and I lived in Leonia.

Dr. Scamardella was an old fashioned doctor, one who once made house calls and had moved to Teaneck when there were still cows in the fields. He literally saved my life. He kept changing the dressings and trying remedies. He didn't know what it was. At first he thought it was a boil. Only when the flesh eating properties of the venom became apparent did he look up spider bites in his medical book and identify the culprit. By then, I had turned the corner.

I was in a new job; I couldn't take time off to be sick and had no medical insurance. For a while I could barely sit, but I showed up every day for work. I am glad the doc didn't know what it was at first. He would have been advised to hospitalize me.

I found out how strong I really am and what I can do if I have to and even if I just want to.

During my career, I worked in kindergartens, nursery schools and day care centers in various parts of New Jersey and in all the boroughs of New York City except the Bronx. I am proud that I did an important job for members of the human family.

I was in a "helping profession" even when, in my fifties, I decided that I couldn't afford to stay in Early Childhood Education anymore and took a job as a Preventive Services Social Worker at New York Foundling Hospital, Staten Island. I was looking forward to retirement and had no pension or medical coverage. I was single and didn't expect to have anyone to help me pay the bills if I got old alone.

I was already living in Staten Island. I had started the "Busy Beach" day care center on the South Beach Psychiatric Center grounds. It was, and is, the result of cooperation between the hospital's unions and its management.

Of course when a union tried to organize the day care workers, the hospital didn't like it. I was offered membership in the union, I was happy, but I wasn't there long enough to get its benefits.

Being the head of any enterprise is probably difficult. I know that heading a day care center is. For one thing, you are the only one with credentials and training in the subject, but everyone, especially if they have achieved parenthood, thinks they know more than you do.

I would last about five years in a job and then something would change. Most day care is "private, nonprofit" and run by a board largely made up of parents. As their children move out of the program, they move on. That means that the board that loved you when they hired you and supported you, is not the same one you are dealing with five years down the line.

I lost jobs but always had glowing letters from someone in the leadership that helped me get another quickly. It worked out in the long run, because changing jobs was the only way to any kind of economic upward mobility.

I considered getting a PhD when I lost my job at Hartley House in Manhattan. (The Health Department wanted the 100 year old stair rail modified and the old guy who was Executive Director wanted none of it. I was the messenger that got "killed" in that one.)

Anyway, I tried but I didn't get into the Fordham program I wanted on the first try and by then I figured out that the unemployment line I was on was full of PhDs. I would have "over qualified" myself.

Well, I was 55 when I took the job at New York Foundling in Staten Island and I was able to stay long enough to get a small pension and retire at 65.

My dad died in February 1991. I took the job in March. I met my wonderful hubby in September of the same year. Things have a way of working out.

Chapter Nineteen

Love At Last

In 1986 I moved to Staten Island because I was working at "Busy Beach". The landlord who lived downstairs in Weehawken wanted the apartment for his recently married daughter. All my daughters had moved on.

I took a very nice apartment on the ground floor of a two family house in a very suburban neighborhood. My landlady, a widow, lived upstairs. She kept the place immaculate and I loved the view of her backyard out of my window.

I loved being back in my city and I loved the small town feel of Staten Island.

It wasn't long before I looked into opportunities to date again. There was no computer dating. The fear of AIDS loomed over the singles